Human Resource Book for Beginners and New Businesses

Simple Principles and Practices for (HR) Dummies

By

Francis A. Wiles

Human Resource Book for Beginners and New
Businesses

About the Author

Francis A. Wiles is an enthusiastic business coach and expert who is committed to enabling people and companies to experience extraordinary growth. Francis uses his extensive knowledge and awareness of the constantly changing business world to help his clients succeed by providing them with inspirational advice and strategic insights. Francis is well-known for his engaging coaching approach and for fusing his dedication to encouraging creativity and adaptability with real-world experience. Because of his unshakable faith in the potential of every company, he offers customized solutions that provide entrepreneurs the skills they need to overcome obstacles and turn their ideas into profitable businesses. The goal of Francis A. Wiles is to mentor and encourage people as they pursue business achievement

Copyright

Disclaimer

The data in this "Human Resource Book for Beginners and New Businesses" is solely meant to be used for general informative purposes. The author and publisher do not make any express or implied claims or assurances on the availability, accuracy, suitability, completeness, or reliability of the information provided herein, despite having taken every precaution to ensure its accuracy and completeness. Any decisions made in reliance on the information in this guide, or for any errors or omissions in the content, are the sole responsibility of the author and publisher.

Human Resource Book for Beginners and New Businesses

INTRODUCTION

Importance of Human Resources for Beginners

In the fast-paced world of business, Human Resources (HR) stands out as a critical component, similar to the lifeblood that keeps an organization running. Understanding the deep relevance of human resources for new entrepreneurs is analogous to unlocking the secret to long-term success.

Fundamentally, human resources serves as a company's pulse, overseeing the complex dance of its diverse personnel. Recognizing the need of nurturing and supporting their staff is critical for growing businesses. It's more than just recruiting; it's about building a community that drives the firm forward.

During the early stages, HR takes on the role of architect, shaping the company culture. It establishes the foundation for workplace principles, standards, and a group identity. A good and inclusive culture, maintained by HR, becomes the fertile soil for employee happiness and, subsequently, heightened productivity.

Furthermore, HR serves as a compass, leading firms through the complicated landscape of employment rules and regulations. For novices, navigating this legal landscape can be difficult without the assistance of HR professionals who ensure compliance, mitigate potential risks, and avoid legal errors.

Recruitment, another key component of human resources, is analogous to carefully selecting the building pieces of a business. Beginners may underestimate the complexity of writing attractive job descriptions and performing good interviews. HR, on the other hand, serves as a skilled storyteller, conveying the company's narrative in order to attract the best people.

HR plays an increasingly important role as firms grow. It becomes the guardian of employee development, directing training activities and encouraging ongoing learning. HR transforms people into valuable assets, armed with the capabilities required to move the organization ahead.

In essence, for new entrepreneurs, human resources serves as a compass, architect, and storyteller. It supports a company's survival and growth by prioritizing its people, realizing that success is a team effort rather than a single endeavor. As a novice, understanding the importance of HR is analogous to recognizing the beating heart within the corporate body, a heart that, when cared for, guarantees the entire system thrives.

CHAPTER 1:

Foundational Concepts

Understanding HR Basics

Understanding the fundamentals of human resources (HR) is equivalent to grasping the critical framework that underpins the entire organizational structure. For individuals new to the profession or in the early phases of a business initiative, learning about HR fundamentals gives a solid foundation for understanding the important functions that contribute to a flourishing workplace.

1. Definition and Scope: Human resources (HR) is the department in charge of managing an organization's human capital. This includes a wide range of tasks, from recruitment and onboarding to employee relations, performance management, and more. Essentially, HR is in charge of the employee experience.

2. Key Functions: HR's varied job can be reduced to a few main functions:

- **Recruitment and Hiring:** Finding, attracting, and hiring the right people.
- **Onboarding:** Assisting new hires in assimilating into the business culture.
- **Employee Relations:** Overseeing workplace dynamics and addressing problems.
- **Performance Management:** Establishing expectations, giving feedback, and encouraging ongoing progress.

- **Training and Development:** Improving employees' skills through learning activities.

- **Benefits Administration:** Manages employee benefits such as health insurance and retirement schemes.

- **Legal Compliance:** Ensuring compliance with employment laws and regulations.

3. Employee Lifecycle Management: HR is involved in the entire employee lifecycle, from recruitment to retirement. This comprehensive approach includes not just bringing new talent on board, but also supporting continuing development, managing performance, and dealing with organizational disruptions.

4. Communication and Confidentiality: Effective communication is crucial for HR. HR practitioners must strike a balance between transparency and secrecy, keeping open channels of communication while respecting individuals' privacy and handling sensitive material with prudence.

5. Organizational Culture: HR plays a crucial role in developing and maintaining organizational culture. This includes setting values, creating a pleasant work atmosphere, and instilling a sense of belonging in employees.

6. Ability to adapt and solve problems: Given the changing nature of the workplace, HR practitioners must be flexible problem solvers. They negotiate issues like disagreements, staffing changes, and changing industrial landscapes with an emphasis on developing solutions that correspond with company objectives.

Furthermore , knowing HR fundamentals is like opening the door to efficient people management. It entails understanding the subtle interaction of functions that lead to a pleasant and productive workplace. Whether in recruitment, employee relations, or compliance, a strong understanding of HR basics enables individuals to make substantial contributions to an organization's success and well-being.

Definition and Scope of Human Resources

Organizations rely heavily on Human Resource Management (HRM) to manage their most precious asset, their human capital. Effective people management requires a variety of tasks and responsibilities, which are included in the scope of HRM. The strategic approach to managing an organization's workforce is known as human resource management. It entails finding, vetting, employing, and orienting staff members in addition to overseeing their performance, growth, and general welfare. Human resource management (HRM) also includes employee relations, benefits, pay, and legal compliance in the workplace.

Essential Roles of Human Resource Administration

Every organization needs Human Resources (HR) to perform a number of critical tasks. These include finding talent, assessing performance, encouraging development and improving skills, and much more. Understanding the notion of Human Resource Management (HRM) is crucial for obtaining a thorough understanding of the roles and responsibilities of HR. The following are Human Resource Management's (HRM) seven main functions:

1. Hiring and Selecting Employees: Finding and hiring the best talent for the company is one of HRM's main goals. This includes creating job descriptions, posting job openings, reviewing resumes, holding interviews, and choosing the best applicants. Building a talented and diversified staff requires effective recruitment and selection procedures.

2. Education and Training: HRM is concerned with improving workers' abilities and proficiencies through training and development initiatives. These programs assist staff members in learning new skills, enhancing their output, and adjusting to shifting corporate requirements. To promote ongoing learning and development within the company, HR experts assess training needs, create training programs, and oversee their effective execution.

3. Management of Performance: HRM is essential to managing worker performance. It entails establishing performance standards, carrying out frequent assessments, giving feedback, and acknowledging accomplishments. Performance management systems support employee development and productivity while assisting in coordinating personal ambitions with corporate aims.

4. Salary and Perquisites Supervisory: HRM includes the planning, implementation, and management of benefit and pay plans. HR specialists ensure that workers receive competitive and equitable pay packages that include wages, bonuses, and other incentives in addition to benefits like health insurance, retirement plans, and paid time off. Employee retention and satisfaction are positively correlated with efficient pay and benefits administration.

5. Engagement and Relations with Employees:

A pleasant workplace requires maintaining good employee interactions. HRM is centered on managing conflict, encouraging open communication, and creating positive working relationships between management and staff. Initiatives to improve job satisfaction, motivation, and staff engagement are also included, as these will boost output and contribute to the success of the company.

6. Safety and Health: HR specialists provide guidelines and protocols to guarantee adherence to workplace safety and health laws. To stop mishaps, injuries, and illnesses linked to the job, they undertake risk assessments, put safety training into practice, and encourage employee wellbeing.

7. Information Management for HR: Another crucial aspect of HRM is the administration of personnel data and HR information systems. HR specialists manage payroll procedures, keep up-to-date personal information, and use HRIS (Human Resource Information Systems) to make administrative work easier. Strategic workforce planning and effective decision-making are supported by well-managed HR information management.

The obligations imposed on HR professionals

An efficient human resources department is essential to building a strong organizational structure and fulfilling business needs by managing your most precious asset, which is your workforce. The Human Resources department comprises multiple disciplines, and HR managers are principally accountable for three primary domains: guaranteeing adherence to legal and ethical norms, fostering a hospitable and diverse work atmosphere, and skillfully managing emergencies and executing modifications.

- **Ensuring adherence to the law and moral principles:** HR specialists are essential in guaranteeing adherence to employment rules, labor legislation, and moral principles. They maintain a current understanding of legal requirements, create policies that conform to legal frameworks, and guarantee that workers are treated fairly and morally. This duty aids in shielding the company and its employees from moral and legal dilemmas.

- **Promoting a Happy and Inclusionary Workplace Environment:** It is the duty of HR specialists to create a welcoming workplace that values equality, diversity, and inclusiveness. They design programs to stop discrimination, encourage tolerance, and foster a cooperative and team-oriented culture. HR specialists also handle employee complaints and assist in settling disputes, fostering a positive work environment for everybody.

- **Managing Change and Crises:** HR experts are vital to the efficient management of organizational transitions in times of crisis or change. They assist in minimizing the impact on the workforce, convey changes, and offer support to staff. HR specialists play the role of change agents, easing staff transitions and assisting them in adjusting to new situations. The field of human resource management is vast and includes a range of duties and obligations inside a business. HRM is crucial in determining the success and well-being of the organization and its workforce, from hiring and selection to training and development, performance management to employee relations, and legal compliance to crisis management. Organizations may foster an atmosphere that develops talent, boosts productivity, and encourages sustainable growth by realizing the importance of HRM and all of its varied functions.

Human Resource Book for Beginners and New Businesses

CHAPTER 2: Legal Framework

The Value of Being Aware of HR Legal Issues

There has never been a more significant function for human resources in the workplace. HR practitioners need to be well-versed in both current and pertinent HR law, in addition to performing the customary tasks of payroll, onboarding, L&D, and recruitment. These HR employment rules guard against harassment and discriminatory behaviors by regulating recruiting and firing procedures, workplace safety, perks and compensation, and confidentiality. They also offer advice in the event of complaints or conflicts at work.

Legal Compliance with HR

Employers and employees are both protected by HR legislation, and businesses must adhere to the rules that regulate the working environment. Policies and procedures that align state and federal legislation with an organization's strategy and objectives must be implemented. A failure to stay current on new HR rules may incur fines, penalties, and in certain situations, legal action.

Understanding these rules is essential for any firm since non-compliance can harm a company's reputation. Since laws differ between states and jurisdictions, this can be difficult. Companies need to keep an eye out for any changes to the law and adjust their policies and processes accordingly. All staff members need to be properly informed about these policies in order for them to know their rights and for the business as a whole to have a unified goal.

Managing Human Resources: Duties

Every compliance issue is familiar to and experienced by an efficient HR manager. These cover matters including labor rights, confidentiality, health and safety, leave entitlements, discrimination and harassment, and employee perks and remuneration.

It is imperative that they are aware of all regulations pertaining to human resource management. They must also be able to create and execute internal policies that take these legal obligations into account. In the case that a current or former employee files a complaint or lawsuit, they also need to be informed of standard operating protocols and policies. Selecting the best candidate for this role not only guarantees adherence to regulations but also enhances the company's overall performance.

How Is Human Resource Management Affected by HR Law?

Every facet of human resource management is impacted by HR law. HR specialists need to be up to date on legal developments. To guarantee workplace compliance, HR has a responsibility to proactively examine and update internal policies. State-specific human resources regulations in the US must be followed in addition to federal laws that have an impact on HRM. There are a number of common protected employee rights, even though the latter vary depending on the employee's location. These include the freedom to create and join unions, the right to privacy, nondiscrimination and equal work opportunities, and basic requirements for terms and conditions of employment. With so many different legal obligations, it's simple to forget how important it is to keep up to date on regulations and regularly modify workplace policies.

While some businesses choose to contract and retain the best candidate for the position, others choose to outsource these responsibilities. Compliance needs to be the first priority in all business decisions, regardless of the course of action your organization has taken. Failing to do so may have consequences such as fines, legal action, reputational harm, and lost revenue.

What HR Professionals Should Know About Employment Law

A business can take many steps to stay abreast of these modifications and steer clear of HR legal complacency:

- Take the initiative and plan ahead for legal changes.
- Stay informed about impending government initiatives and be mindful of how they might affect internal policies and processes.
- Perform audits on a regular basis.
- In order to guarantee HR regulatory compliance across all company domains, create checklists and periodically review them.

- To encourage accountability and ownership, designate specific policy owners within the HR division.

- To keep informed about upcoming changes to regulations affecting human resources management, attend frequent seminars and webinars.

- Give HR staff regular training on employment law.

- Emphasize on staff members the value of adhering to internal policies and procedures.

- HR professionals should proactively implement policies that correspond with modifications in employment laws.

- Steer clear of cost-benefit evaluations of the expenses related to compliance. The amount of money needed to assure compliance will be significantly less than what a business could lose via fines and legal action.

Plan/Avoid/Defend

In addition to the aforementioned, the US Department of Labor (DOL) has put in place a program to assist businesses in making sure they adhere to all legal requirements for HR experts.

Employers in the US are the objective of the Plan/Prevent/Protect campaign, which was launched in 2010. In order to address human resources law compliance issues that are under the jurisdiction of the Wage and Hour Division (WHD), the Office of Federal Contract Compliance Programs (OFCCP), the Mine Safety and Health Administration (MSHA), and the Occupational Safety and Health

Administration (OSHA), businesses are required to create Compliance Action Plans.

Companies are encouraged to recognize and reduce the risk of non-compliance by the DOL enforcement strategy. It also emphasizes how crucial it is to put policies into place at every level of a company in order to reduce the possibility of legal infractions. In order to make sure the goals of the plan are being achieved, a well-designed plan should also contain routine monitoring and audits. You may reduce the likelihood of compliance problems for your business by implementing an efficient compliance plan. Furthermore, you contribute to the development of a corporate culture that is dedicated to attaining compliance throughout the working environment. In order to relieve pressure on the HR department, it's also critical

to establish accountability at the departmental
and employee levels.

Federal Laws Are the Main Human Resources Laws

It can be difficult for HR managers to stay
current with the rules pertaining to human
resources. There are a ton of updates at the
municipal, state, and federal levels with every
new year. Basic HR regulations control salaries,
benefits, and pensions. Working circumstances
are impacted by legislation pertaining to
occupational safety and health. Tax laws, such as
those pertaining to stock purchase plans and
employee profit sharing, have an impact on
compensation. In addition, in light of the current
#metoo movement, HR discrimination and

harassment regulations are more crucial than ever.

There are some federal laws that apply to every part of the country, notwithstanding differences based on state and jurisdiction.

HRM's Federal Legal Concerns

- America's federal safety net for the elderly, jobless, and underprivileged was established by the Social Security Act of 1935. The primary requirement of the initial Social Security Act was to provide retirees over 65 with financial benefits based on their lifetime payroll tax contributions.

- Fair work Standards Act (1938): establishes overtime compensation, prohibits child work, and sets the federal minimum wage, which is periodically increased by Congress.

- Known also as the Wagner Act, the National Labor Relations Act was passed in 1935. permits unionization of employees and outlaws unfair labor practices by employers.

- The Equal Pay Act of 1963 does away with gender-based wage disparities. aimed to abolish the practice of paying women less for the same job because of their gender when it was signed into law by John F. Kennedy.

- Employment discrimination on the basis of race, color, religion, gender, or national origin is prohibited by the Civil Rights Act of 1964.

- The Age Discrimination Act of 1967 forbids discrimination based on age against those who are older than 40.

- Occupational Safety and Health Act (1970): This law guarantees a workplace free from hazards and safeguards the health and safety of employees.

- The Americans with Disabilities Act (1990) forbids discrimination in the workplace on the grounds of physical or mental impairments.

- Employers are required by the 1993 Family and Medical Leave Act to offer unpaid leave in the event of illness, adoption, or childbirth.

- Retirement Income Security Act (1974): Protects individuals by establishing minimal requirements for the majority of voluntarily organized retirement and health plans in the private sector.

Compliance with HR: Challenges for Human Resources

As we've covered, in order to guarantee compliance with labor regulations pertaining to HR, an HR professional must be knowledgeable of a number of legal issues. The following are some of the most important HR legislation that affect HR:

Laws Governing Employee Time Tracking: One of the main responsibilities of HR is tracking time and attendance. Therefore, it's critical to ensure that HR managers are following all applicable legal guidelines for employee time monitoring. Does a federal statute regarding timesheets exist? The Federal Labor Standards Act (FLSA) mandates that records contain the day and time of employees' start and end of work shifts, in addition to the total number of hours worked per day and week. Additional guidelines on the tracking of employee hours and the allocation of overtime or time-in-lieu may be provided by state law.

Keep Information Private: A wide range of private employee data is accessible to the HR division. This can contain job contracts, personal addresses and phone numbers, health details, tax and social security numbers, and more. It is necessary to protect this personal information in order to comply with data protection laws.

Additionally, HR is responsible for maintaining the privacy of information about company and management strategy data. Data privacy might provide particular difficulties when it comes to workplace investigations and disciplinary actions. Finding the ideal ratio between openness and privacy is necessary. Make sure your company's policies respect local laws to protect data privacy.

Benefits for Workers: HR managers are responsible for making sure that all workers receive benefits and pay in compliance with federal employment laws. This covers wages, sick pay and yearly leave, pensions (which provide a secure retirement income for employees), and overtime compensation. Contractual salaries must adhere to the Fair Work Act and the minimum pay that has been set. While they are not mandated by law, extra benefits like wellness initiatives and flexible work schedules can encourage staff members and foster a positive work environment.

Discrimination at Work: Laws against workplace discrimination guarantees that workers are shielded from prejudice at all job levels. Recruitment, terms and conditions of employment, training, compensation and benefits, opportunities for promotion and transfer, termination and redundancy are all included in this. Gender, color, sexual orientation, and religion are all possible grounds for discrimination. Employers are required to make sure that there is no discrimination on the basis of veteran status, handicap, or marital and family status. Anti-discrimination legislation must be complied with by all company activities. An employee has the right to file a discrimination case if they believe they were the victim of discrimination and were dealt with unfairly, such as being fired or not promoted.

Employers must also advise staff members of their legal rights under EEOC regulations. Workers need to understand that filing a discrimination complaint has no bearing on their job security or working conditions.

Mistreatment: Preventing harassment is a significant legal concern in the field of human resources. Businesses need to implement anti-harassment procedures that aim to establish and preserve a workplace where employees are treated with respect, decency, and dignity. All employees, whether new and old, must have easy access to these policies. Furthermore, it is imperative that managers receive training to enable them to identify possible instances of harassment and to conduct unbiased, fair, and comprehensive investigations in the event that an employee files a complaint. The metoo movement's growing popularity has contributed to a notable rise in sexual discrimination lawsuits brought to the Equal Employment Opportunity Commission in recent years. As a result, several states have established new laws requiring the implementation of workplace sexual harassment prevention training, such as California and New York State.

Occupational Safety: The human resources division bears the responsibility of guaranteeing a secure working environment for every employee. In addition, they must instill a culture of safety at work and guarantee that all employees receive sufficient instruction and direction on all topics pertaining to health and safety. All relevant data must be recorded, thoroughly examined, and regular risk assessments and other preventative measures must be implemented in the event of an accident or incident.

Workplace Rights: All labor rights must be known to employers. Supervisors are responsible for making sure that pertinent policies and procedures are followed and shared with all staff members. This covers overtime compensation in addition to equal pay. This additional allowance is tracked and computed in accordance with the FLSA and, for waged employees, minimum rates per hour. It also considers rights about pay schedules, breaks, and working hours.

About 180 employee job protection rules, ranging from salary requirements to notice periods for termination and maternity leave benefits, are enforced by the Department of Labor. Other safeguards are overseen by organizations like the U.S. Commission on Equal Employment Opportunity. Employees who are protected by these laws get a minimum wage and are shielded from unfair labor practices.

Obstacles in Recruiting: Hiring international personnel presents hurdles for most HR managers. Although these workers greatly enhance diversity and offer value to an organization, the hiring procedure could be a little more difficult. Employers need to make sure foreign workers are authorized to work in the US by having them fill out form I-9 before hiring them.

Typical HR Lawsuits: If there is non-compliance, an employee has the right to sue for a number of different reasons. It follows that HR departments need to be up to date on all rules and regulations. They also need to know how to respond to any legal difficulties that might come up.

The following are the most typical employee lawsuits in the United States:

- If an employee gets paid less than their agreed pay or bonuses, this constitutes a breach of their employment contract's terms and conditions.
- complaints about discrimination based on sexual orientation, gender, and race
- wrongful dismissal without good cause
- Not fulfilling one's contractual obligations

- Workplace personal injury injuries
- Unpaid overtime as well as non-compliance with FLSA requirements for workers who are not paid salaries.
- harassment, which includes bullying and sexual harassment.

Managing Legal Matters: Preventing Lawsuits

The legal process can be expensive and time-consuming. Therefore, in order to ensure that they minimize all costs, HR departments need to put in place a number of procedures. Making plans to shield your business from future legal problems will guarantee that every employee works in a fair atmosphere and stop any possible problems from turning into lawsuits. To help your business be ready to handle any future accusations, consider the following advice. Defend and safeguard your company from any future legal actions.

Ways to keep employee lawsuits at bay

- Adhere to any modifications to employment laws and regulations while implementing policies and processes.
- Make sure that all policies are communicated to and easily accessible to current staff members.
- As part of the onboarding process for new hires, provide training on corporate policies and procedures.
- Make sure workers understand their rights.
- Managers should receive training so they can see possible problems and take action

to stop a situation from getting worse. This covers instruction on best practices, federal, state, and municipal laws, as well as corporate rules.

- Employees should receive training on safe work practices and workplace safety.
- Keep records of everything, including staff reviews, performance assessments, and attendance logs.
- Make sure that all disciplinary actions have a written trail.
- To guarantee worldwide compliance with HR regulations, keep staff uniformity throughout all tiers of the company.
- Steer clear of favoritism and employee single outs.

- Assure that all workers follow the same guidelines and that all rules and regulations are followed.

- Keep abreast of any modifications to the law, especially those pertaining to the Fair Labor rules Act (FLSA), municipal wage and hour statutes, and other labor rights rules.

- To ensure compliance at all organizational levels, conduct routine audits and develop checklists.

- Keep abreast of all regulatory changes and adhere to these straightforward best practices.

HR managers may contribute to the overall performance of their organizations by assisting in ensuring compliance, shielding their businesses from avoidable workplace accidents, and averting potentially expensive legal actions.

Overview of Employment Laws

The legal framework that controls the interaction between employers and employees and guarantees equitable treatment, rights, and obligations at work is known as employment laws. This summary offers a quick look at important areas of employment law that employers, human resources specialists, and workers need to be aware of.

1. Equal Employment Opportunity (EEO): EEO rules forbid discrimination on the basis of age, handicap, race, color, religion, sex, national origin, or genetic information. The goal is to

establish a work environment where everyone
has an equal chance to achieve.

2. Fair Labor Standards Act (FLSA): FLSA
sets minimum wage, eligibility for overtime
compensation, recordkeeping requirements, and
child labor laws. It sets rules for working hours
and guarantees that workers receive just
compensation for their labor.

3. Family and Medical Leave Act (FMLA):
The FMLA allows qualifying workers to take up
to 12 weeks of unpaid leave annually for certain
medical or family-related reasons, such as a
major illness, the birth or adoption of a child, or
providing care for a family member who is ill.

**4. Occupational Safety and Health Act
(OSHA):** OSHA requires employers to provide

a safe and healthy work environment. Employers must offer a safe working environment free from known risks, educate staff on safety procedures, and keep track of any illnesses or injuries sustained at work.

5. The Americans with Disabilities Act (ADA): The ADA forbids discrimination against disabled people in the workplace. Employers are required to provide individuals with impairments with reasonable accommodations so they can perform their job duties.

6. The Civil Rights Act's Title VII: This section forbids discrimination in the workplace on the grounds of race, color, religion, sex, or national origin. It includes hiring, promoting, and terminating employees, among other employment procedures, and is applicable to companies with at least 15 workers.

7. Age Discrimination in Employment Act (ADEA): The ADEA safeguards people forty years of age and above from age-based discrimination in the workplace. It covers hiring, promotion, pay, and other employment procedures and is applicable to companies with 20 or more workers.

8. The NLRA, or National Labor Relations Act: The NLRA safeguards workers' rights to collective bargaining, the creation or membership in labor unions, and coordinated actions for protection and assistance. It lays down rules for how labor unions and employers should interact.

9. Employment Retirement Income Security Act (ERISA): ERISA establishes guidelines for welfare and pension schemes that companies offer. It sets rules for plan management and guarantees the preservation of employees' rights to promised benefits.

Having a fair and legally compliant workplace requires understanding and adherence to various employment rules. There may be legal repercussions for noncompliance, which could harm the employer's finances and image. In order to assure compliance, firms should stay up to date on changes to employment regulations and consult a lawyer.

Human Resource Book for Beginners and New
Businesses

CHAPTER 3:

Recruitment and Hiring

Recruitment and hiring are like putting together a puzzle within a firm, with each new member contributing a distinctive piece to the overall picture. The approach begins with developing a job description that extends beyond duties and serves as an invitation to become a part of the bigger picture.

Strategic sourcing and intelligent job listings lay the groundwork for identifying the right components - the ideal candidates. Interviews are similar to integrating these elements into the existing composition, ensuring they mix seamlessly. It's not only about abilities; it's about finding someone whose contribution is in line with the company's mission.

Once the necessary components are found, the onboarding process transitions into the assembly phase, assisting new personnel in seamlessly integrating into the existing picture. The goal is to create a united image that moves the organization forward, with each employee contributing to the overall success story.

Effective Job Descriptions

- Crafting an effective job description is similar to painting a vivid picture of a role; you want potential candidates to perceive themselves as an integral component of the canvas. It's more than just listing tasks; it's about producing an enticing snapshot that piques attention and fits with the company's culture.

- Begin with a clear and simple title that conveys the essence of the role. The introduction should be interesting, providing a glimpse into the fascinating potential that the role offers. Consider it the first stroke on the canvas, laying the groundwork for everything follows.

- Clearly outline responsibilities, including the day-to-day tasks involved. However, don't forget to emphasize the overall impact - illustrate how each activity fits into the wider vision. Consider it as adding layers and colors to the painting to create depth and dimension.

- Be realistic with your qualifications. Specify must-haves and nice-to-haves to ensure that candidates understand the core abilities while still giving possibility for advancement. This is analogous to choosing the perfect tones for your artwork: a combination that complements the entire composition.

- End the explanation with a call to action that encourages potential candidates to participate in the canvas. It's the final touch that motivates people to see themselves in the role and take the next step.

Remember that a great job description is more than simply a list; it is an artistic depiction of an opportunity that entices the right people to add their own colors to your team's canvas.

Recruitment Strategies for New Businesses

Every company strives to have the greatest employees. To accomplish this effectively, you must have a recruitment strategy in place that allows you to identify, hire, and retain employees. Of course, there are other ways to recruit talent. In this post, we will look at the most effective recruitment tactics employed in today's industry. Understanding talent acquisition and how it works is critical to building an effective recruitment strategy. Here are ten recruitment methods you may use right away.

Here are ten successful recruitment tactics for businesses:

1. Define your corporate brand: When people think about places to work, they frequently start with well-known companies that they recognize and trust. Your brand is built on the reputation you have for your products and services. If someone is unfamiliar with your brand, you can profit by creating an effective About Us page on your website. This should clearly explain your company's goal and mission, as well as an interesting synopsis of your story. Consider why individuals would want to work for your company, how diverse your staff is, and whether current employees endorse it as a good place to work.

2. Treat candidates like customers: Great talent wants to work in an environment that values professionalism. One of the finest ways to express this is through the recruitment process. Just as you would respect your customers' time, you should do the same with applicants. Set a time limit for an interview or phone conversation, communicate it to the candidate, and stick to it. When a candidate arrives to meet with you, take the time to offer them a drink and show them where the restrooms are. This hospitality goes a long way toward establishing confidence. After the interview, make yourself available for follow-up inquiries by providing your contact information.

3. Use Social Media in a Targeted Approach: You probably use social media to attract clients, but you can also use it to find new employees.

On social media, publish job openings and answer questions about available roles. Great talent is frequently discovered among those who are already familiar with and follow your brand. Also, make sure that your company's social media presence reflects everything it does, including non-business activities. If you support nonprofits or charities, publish posts with images about them. This allows applicants to associate themselves with you in a way that makes them feel good about the work they will be doing under your direction.

4. Create job ads that reflect your company: Your company's culture is crucial, and your job descriptions should reflect this. If lighthearted fun is part of the culture, include it in the job advertisement. If everything is business at the office, make sure the advertisement looks professional and polished. Applicants will be drawn to work for the company based on how the advertisement reads, and you will be delighted you allowed your company personality shine through so that you can attract those who will fit into your corporate culture.

5. Implement an employee referral program: If you already have a terrific team of employees, you can probably trust their recommendations for prospective hires. Good people usually know and hang out with other good people, and they will recommend people who fit into the company's culture. A referral program incentivizes them to approach friends and potential applicants about working for you. You may even go beyond an incentive and turn the referral process into a contest with interesting prizes and awards for participants.

6. Implement an applicant tracking system:
Hiring managers can use applicant tracking tools
to better manage the recruitment and hiring
process. Recruiting software can help companies
save time and money when they are continually
recruiting. Make sure the software automates the
job posting and candidate identification
processes. Great software may also aid with
candidate sorting, appointment scheduling, and
new hire onboarding.

7. Utilize niche job boards: Sometimes you
have to look beyond the box to locate the
appropriate talent. This could entail going to
specialist job forums where the right candidates
congregate. These will automatically eliminate
the bulk of possible applicants that aren't a good

fit anyway. Check the websites of professional groups to see if they have a job board where you can list your position. In most circumstances, doing so will result in a higher-quality lead.

8. Make interviews engaging: It is easy to fall into the trap of questioning people throughout the interview process. You're trying to acquire specific information while keeping to a timetable. However, this does not effectively engage elite talent. To get them involved in the process, ask them questions and solicit comments. Give them access to current staff and participate in the dialog yourself. By doing so, you will help your organization stand out and attract the proper individuals.

9. Use Recruiting Videos: A recruiting film can assist prospective employees understand the company's mission and culture. You can take a few minutes to explain this and the job before the candidate walks in the door. This will assist in vetting people who wish to join the company.

10. Reach out to previous applicants: While there may be reasons why you did not hire someone previously, reaching out to past prospects might provide you with an excellent pool of talent for various positions. Furthermore, you never know when someone will develop new qualities or skills that would be a terrific fit for you right now. Have your hiring manager mark prospects who don't get hired as persons you like and want to keep in touch. This will allow you to traverse the hiring process more efficiently.

How Can Recruiting Software Help?

Recruiting software is a tool that assists hiring managers in creating job advertisements, finding qualified candidates, and onboarding the final selections. It automates several hiring processes, such as automatically posting job advertising on relevant job sites. It will also assist the recruiter in sorting through the applications and categorizing them based on their interests. Once in the system, applicants can be invited for an interview.

Hiring managers utilize recruiting software not only during the recruiting process, but also to manage new personnel. Once an offer is made, great recruiting software automates onboarding with the appropriate documents and videos to help get the latest recruit into the system and comply with the requirements. To improve your recruiting efforts, make sure you're more than just an interviewer. Be an evangelist for the company, showing others why they should join the team. Using efficient recruitment tactics can allow you to locate the ideal personnel in the shortest amount of time.

Interviewing Techniques for Beginners

When conducting interviews with new candidates, treat them as genuine conversations rather than checklists. Here are some friendly ways to make those chats more insightful:

1. Unveiling Experiences: Begin with questions that prompt candidates to share experiences from their previous employment. It's about peeling back the layers of their career journey to discover what drives them.

2. Active Listening: Pay attention not just to the words, but also to their tone and energy. It is about determining the candidate's actual mood beyond what is openly said.

3. Checking Compatibility: Discuss values, work styles, and teamwork approaches. You want to ensure that their approach is consistent with the team dynamics.

4. talents Showcase: Request candidates to demonstrate their talents using real-world examples. It's like inviting people to demonstrate their strengths and abilities in a variety of situations.

5. Open Exploration: Ask open-ended questions to encourage candidates to reveal more. It is about inviting them to deliver a thorough perspective rather than a concise response.

6. Reality Preview: Provide practical information about the job. This is about providing an accurate preview so they have a good picture of what the role entails.

7. Diverse Perspectives: Use multiple interviewees to provide a diversified conversation. It's about getting multiple perspectives to ensure a comprehensive grasp of the prospect.

8. In-Depth Inquiry: If a candidate raises an interesting issue, explore deeper. It's about delving into intriguing areas of their lives and opinions.

9. Hypothetical Scenarios: Ask candidates to navigate hypothetical situations relevant to the role. It involves evaluating their inventiveness and problem-solving abilities in hypothetical settings.

10. Non-Verbal Communication: Pay attention to nonverbal indicators including body language and facial expressions. It is about understanding the conversation's unspoken parts in addition to verbal responses.

Remember that an interview is a mutual exploration. You're not simply looking for the best fit for your team; candidates are also looking for a place where they can make a meaningful contribution. Make it an authentic and interesting conversation to ensure a good fit for everyone involved.

CHAPTER 4: Onboarding and Training

Onboarding and training act as a welcome handshake and road map for new team members as they join an organization. Starting with onboarding, the idea is to foster a sense of belonging rather than simply completing paperwork. Introducing them to the company's culture and values allows for a smooth transition.

Training, on the other hand, is a masterclass where employees develop their skills. It is more than just learning the ropes; it is about developing skills that will enable them to make a significant contribution. Training transforms them into valuable contributors, preparing them to face the exciting path ahead. Onboarding and training work together to create a workforce that is not just skilled but also seamlessly integrated into the company's success rhythm.

Structured onboarding processes

A successful company relies on its people to drive growth and meet organizational objectives. However, many businesses underestimate the value of a well-organized staff onboarding process. The initial period of employment is crucial for increasing employee engagement, productivity, and overall well-being. Organizations may nurture their new hires by adopting a well-structured onboarding process that includes pre-boarding activities, a welcome first day, complete orientation, mentorship, and ongoing support.

1. Ease of Transition and Reduced Stress:
New jobs can be intimidating and unpleasant for
employees. A planned onboarding procedure
helps to reduce these issues by providing a clear
path for new employees. It ensures that they
have all of the knowledge and resources they
need to understand their roles, responsibilities,
and objectives. Employees gain confidence and
may swiftly adapt to their new surroundings
when full instruction on corporate policies,
procedures, and cultural norms is provided. This
quicker transition not only decreases stress, but
also helps employees retain a happy attitude,
allowing them to concentrate on their work and
overall well-being.

2.   Increased   Employee   Engagement:
Successful organizations rely on engaged employees. A well-structured onboarding process may instill a sense of belonging and dedication from day one. It establishes the foundation for a pleasant employee experience by introducing new employees to the company's culture, values, and mission. During the onboarding process, organizations can emphasize the significance of each employee's contribution to the overarching goals and vision. Organizations may instill a strong sense of purpose and encourage active participation in new hires by giving them opportunities to communicate with their colleagues, supervisors, and company executives. Employees who are engaged are more likely to be motivated, productive, and satisfied, which improves their overall well-being.

3.   Improved   Time   to   Productivity:
Effectiveness is crucial for any firm. A planned
onboarding process speeds up the orientation
and training of new workers, allowing them to
become   productive   faster.   Companies   can
shorten the learning curve by offering clear
employment requirements, access to relevant
resources, and comprehensive training programs.
This not only benefits the firm but also improves
the well-being of new employees. When people
are confident and capable in their roles, they feel
a sense of success and fulfillment. This faster
path to productivity boosts their self-esteem and
well-being.

4. Improved Retention Rates: Employee
turnover   is   costly   and   disrupts   company
harmony.   A   systematic   onboarding   process

fosters a pleasant first impression and a solid link between new employees and their employers. Employees who feel valued, supported, and engaged are more likely to stay loyal and devoted to the firm. Effective onboarding programs can also help new employees form relationships with their coworkers and managers, building a sense of community and belonging.

Furthermore, by providing continual assistance and chances for growth and development, businesses may demonstrate their commitment to employee success. Enhanced retention rates result in a more stable workforce, lower recruitment expenses, and a stronger emphasis on employee well-being.

5. Improved Wellness and Work/Life Balance: A well-structured onboarding process goes beyond just orientation. It can also involve complete wellness efforts that focus on employees' health and work-life balance. Organizations can implement wellness initiatives, provide access to health resources, and promote healthy habits from the start. During onboarding, businesses can present employees to the many wellness options available, such as exercise programs, mental health resources, and stress management approaches. Organizations can also promote work-life balance by implementing rules that encourage flexible scheduling, remote work choices, and time off benefits. Prioritizing employee well-being during onboarding helps firms set the tone for a healthy work environment and lay the groundwork for long-term wellness programs.

Implementing a systematic employee onboarding process is a strategic investment in an organization's performance and well-being, rather than a bureaucratic need. Organizations may build a vibrant work environment that supports success and longevity by smoothing the transition for new hires, increasing employee engagement, reducing time to productivity, improving retention rates, and expanding wellness initiatives. Prioritizing employee onboarding and wellness is an important step in creating a healthier, more productive staff.

Developing Training Programs

Training programs can benefit any workforce when they are properly planned and implemented. They assist employees in developing applicable skills, which may lead to better productivity, a more positive business culture, and lower employee turnover. Learning about training programs can be beneficial if you work in a human resources (HR) department and want to build a program that fits the needs of employees while also meeting the organization's criteria. In this post, we will outline the procedures for creating training programs and examine their significance.

Steps for designing employee training programs

When establishing training programs, all elements must be considered to guarantee that they produce the desired results. This allows you to adjust the training content to achieve your desired results. It also allows you to address any concerns that may arise while presenting the training. Here are seven steps that will help you create an efficient employee training program:

1. Identify training needs: The goal of a training program is to close any knowledge or skill gaps in the workplace. To ensure the program's success, undertake a training needs analysis first. This is a procedure that involves reviewing employees' present performance, comparing it to the desired level, and identifying opportunities for development. For example, following analysis, an education board implementing a new international test may expect its workers to understand how to give and monitor the exam.

2. Define learning objectives: It is critical to explicitly define what you expect staff to do after the training. You may be aiming to improve their language proficiency or abilities in a certain area. Defining your learning aim allows you to develop content that helps employees progress towards a desired outcome. When defining goals for a training program, it is critical to ensure that your objectives are measurable. You can accomplish this by using a specified, measurable, attainable, reasonable, and time-based (SMART) or objectives and key results (OKR) framework.

3. Understand various training strategies: Learning styles determine how well employees understand the training program's subject matter. Using a range of training strategies to keep staff engaged throughout the program is critical. Case studies, instructor-led training, coaching, hands-on training, group training, and management-specific training are some of the several training options available, depending on the employees' learning style and program content.

Pre-training study may be required at this point to find the optimal strategy. You can identify learning types by having employees fill out a questionnaire or observing their behavior. You can also perform a pre-training survey to determine their familiarity of the course subject.

4. Create training content: You can start creating your material by using the information you gathered throughout your pre-training study. Before you begin generating any training material, you should create a plan that will help you in keeping your content useful, current, and organized. It's a good idea to double-check that your focus is on the employees' learning needs, rather than what is convenient for the trainer. Here are some more tips for generating training content:

- Break down each topic systematically to lay the groundwork for the next session. This also allows employees to have a better knowledge of the subject.

- Include training materials that empower employees to take control of their own learning.

- Ensure that there are interactive and hands-on components that allow employees to collaborate.

- Combine diverse forms to make your training interesting. Monitoring which formats employees engage with the most can assist enhance future training programs.

- To make your training more relatable, use appropriate real-life examples.

- Create an area for feedback as the training session progresses.

5. Prepare the training materials: A training program is generally made up of multiple modules. These modules may offer content using a variety of materials. It's critical that you select the type that will assist you attain your training goals. The following are samples of various training materials:

- PowerPoint presentations
- Charts or graphs
- Reading materials, such as brochures, booklets, and handouts.
- e-learning links for additional research and training activities.
- appropriate log-in information for online training activities
- physical resources for hands-on training activities.

6. Conduct the training: Attendance is an important factor in the effectiveness of a training program. It is critical to ensure that staff understand the necessity of attending training and whether or not registration is required. This allows you to properly plan the program and avoid last-minute preparations. Before the training begins, you can prepare employees by discussing the approach or mix of methods you will use to deliver the training.

You can also provide them guidance for what to do before, during, and after the training. If you intend to evaluate how much they learnt at the end of the training, you must inform them of how you intend to do so before the program begins.

7. Evaluate the program: Conducting an evaluation at the end of a training session allows you to determine its effectiveness. This necessitates revisiting your goals and determining whether or not you were successful in meeting them. Here are some factors to consider when measuring the success of training: Training Feedback: You can get feedback on the success of the training by simply asking attendees or conducting an anonymous online poll. Examine the responses to see if they appreciated the strategy you employed and learnt something, as well as what their overall thoughts or suggestions are for the program.

- **Knowledge gained:** Tests, quizzes, and demonstrations can assist you determine how effectively the team understands the subject you gave. It can also be an engaging method for them to reflect on what they've learnt.

- **Goals were met:** Check the first learning objectives to see if you met them. You can accomplish this by remeasuring a SMART objective or observing employees to determine if they are utilizing the new knowledge or skills they learned during the training.

- **Quantifiable business outcomes:** The training is effective if you notice any changes in the workplace during the next quarter that you can attribute to it. These adjustments could result in higher production or more income for the organization.

Importance of Developing an Employee Training Program

While creating a training program takes time and work, it is essential for the success of any organization. This program is an investment that provides several personal and professional benefits. Here are some benefits of training employees:

Develop knowledge and skills: When employees join in training programs, they can gain knowledge and skills that will help them improve their individual work performance. They may develop communication, problem-solving, project management, strategic thinking, active listening, and crisis management abilities as they collaborate on training activities.

These talents benefit both people and the firm as a whole.

Establish workplace ties: Employees frequently connect on a deeper level when they are brought together to increase their skills and expertise. Team exercises empower them to share ideas and collaborate to attain goals. Learning from one another's strengths and addressing problems jointly can result in a strong and cohesive workforce that benefits both team members and the organization.

Create future leaders: Employers frequently consider candidates who actively participate in their training programs for managerial roles. Training programs make a significant contribution to employee development, preparing individuals to take on leadership roles within a business. The best managers are typically those who are already members of the organization, understand its goal, and can inspire other employees to work toward the company's growth. Their familiarity of the organization provides them with a distinct perspective that new recruits may not have. Training programs address the leadership needs of both employees and organizations.

Keep employees: Training programs are beneficial because they help retain top people, which is critical to a company's sustainability. Potential candidates who can demonstrate participation in training programs may have a better chance of landing a job. Training is a crucial aspect of the recruitment process. It can boost employee value, loyalty, and retention.

Increase productivity: A skilled workforce is a productive one. Teams that routinely meet for training to equip themselves with necessary skills and technical knowledge are more likely to create high-quality work. Employees learn how to be more effective at work as they progress through the company's training programs. If productivity increases, the company progresses. A rise in sales or profit is just one of several measures of a training program's success.

Improve workplace engagement: Training programs can help break up the monotony of work and make it more interesting for employees. Employees who can participate in intellectually stimulating experiences are more likely to be engaged in the workplace and have less idle time. Training programs also urge firms to evaluate employees in a more holistic manner, taking into account both their job responsibilities and their training performance.

CHAPTER 5: Employee Handbook and Policies

The majority of businesses have rules or guidelines controlling their hiring practices, however these are occasionally upheld informally. This may result in uneven implementation and misunderstandings regarding the rights and obligations of employers and employees. These guidelines are formalized in an employee handbook, providing staff members with a printed resource they may peruse and refer to.

When creating a new one or updating an old one, keep these important points in mind. The mission, policies, and expectations of a corporation are outlined in the employee handbook. It guarantees a positive work atmosphere by outlining the rights and obligations of employees. Basic employment information, workplace rules, a code of behavior, pay and benefits, working hours, and termination procedures are all covered in the handbook. Your company's mission, procedures, and expectations are communicated via an employee handbook. Employers provide this to staff members in order to make clear their rights and obligations while working for the company.

You can get started on writing your own document by using this template. The policy in the employee handbook ought to contain:

- **Workplace fundamentals:** An explanation of terms used in the workplace, guidelines for attendance, and a rundown of the hiring procedure

- **Workplace policies:** outlines the conditions of the workplace, such as safety, harassment prevention, and secrecy

- **Code of conduct:** Rules governing how employees should behave, including attire, online safety, conflicts of interest, and interpersonal interactions at work.

You can also change the language in this template to fit the culture of your business.

What ought to be in an employee handbook is as follows: Every key policy included in an employee handbook is covered by this template:

- Workplace Fundamentals
- Workplace Guidelines
- Guidelines for Behavior
- Recompense and advancement
- Advantages and Rewards
- Time Off, Vacation, and PTO
- Termination and Resignation of Employees

These sections can be combined to create a comprehensive employee handbook for your business. These elements are included in the complete template along with an introduction so you may greet new hires at your business.

To boost your efforts even more, below are some recommendations outlining each section and some advice on how to tailor your own employee handbook to your company's needs:

Workplace Fundamentals: This section helps you define some basic terms linked to employment and is primarily instructive. It will help your staff members understand the conditions of their employment and job description. When they have simple inquiries, they can go to this section as a resource.

This is also a good place to establish attendance policies. You might also provide future hiring managers in your organization with an explanation of your recruitment procedure.

The contents of the Employment Basics template are as follows:

- **Types of employment contracts:** Define interns, apprentices, and any individuals you employ in addition to full-time and part-time employees.

- **Employment with equal opportunities:** This declaration is required for legal reasons as well as to foster a meritocracy and respectful atmosphere at work.

- **Recruitment and selection procedure:** Describe the standard procedures you follow when employing new employees.

Define the stage at which recruiting managers can request pre-employment checks and even how to handle them if you perform these checks frequently. Similarly, if you often offer referral prizes or have a permanent referral program, this is a wonderful place to describe the process and any associated policies.

- **Attendance:** The state has regulations about what to do when workers are unable to report to work or in what circumstances unreported absences may be excused.

Workplace Guidelines: This section outlines the ideal and current state of your workplace. It's about the working environment your staff members are in. Incorporate health and safety and anti-harassment regulations into your employee handbook to create a safe and enjoyable work environment where your staff members can flourish.

This template will assist you in creating the Workplace policies section. The following policies are presented, along with advice on how to modify them for your particular workplace:

- **Privacy and data security:** Although our template provides general guidelines for information security, you must adjust it to take into consideration any particular legal requirements that may apply to your business. Talk about these regulations, how you make sure you abide by them, and what you expect of your staff.

- **Violence and harassment:** A positive work environment depends in large part on colleagues treating one another with respect. You can adamantly declare in this part that you will stop harassment and violence in the workplace. Along with outlining potential consequences, you will also clarify what constitutes harassment.

- **Workplace health and safety:** In order to maintain a safe and healthy work environment, employees must abide by the rules outlined in this section. You can include the steps your business has done to abide by laws pertaining to occupational health and safety, safeguard workers in dangerous tasks, and handle crises. Particular sections on smoking cessation, emergency preparedness, and drug-free workplaces are included in our template. If your workplace has appropriate policies in place, you might also include a mental health policy.

Guidelines for Behavior: Employee conduct is outlined in your code of conduct. You will specify how you want workers to interact with coworkers, partners, clients, and other stakeholders. It all comes down to developing a professional and safe environment for all, as well as ethics and trust.

You can use this comprehensive template, which has the following sections, to work on your own code of conduct:

- **Dress code:** Even if your business doesn't have one, you can still list it here. Workers need to be aware of what they can and cannot wear. Provide as much information as you can about the standards; for instance, what does your organization mean by "formal attire"?

- **Digital gadgets and cyber security:** Talk about using business email, company cell phones, the internet, and social media (both personal and professional). Establish rules without being unduly controlling to staff members; most workers anticipate some latitude in these areas, provided security and data protection protocols are adhered to.

- **Conflict of interest:** In this section, you will explain what a conflict of interest is, how employees can resolve one when one arises, and what happens if they intentionally violate any applicable laws or corporate policies.

- **Employee relationships and fraternization:** Although many businesses allow employees to date or form friendships, there are some guidelines that must be followed to prevent unprofessional situations or rumor.

- **Employment of family members:** It's critical to address this issue in order to prevent claims of favoritism and nepotism. Specify the types of working ties that relatives are permitted to have in your organization.

- **Visitors to the workplace:** This concerns both data security and the preservation of company assets. Describe the procedure for inviting guests onto corporate property to ensure that staff members are consistently responsible and alert.

- **Distribution and solicitation:** This section discusses attempts by clients or staff to spread flyers, goods, or services, as well as the actions that staff members can take in these situations.

Recompense and advancement: This section describes how to compensate staff members for their efforts and foster their professional growth. By implementing these policies, you encourage staff members to remain with you by demonstrating your worth to them.

Use this compensation and development template, which includes the following components, to get started on this:

- **Payroll and compensation status:** This section is crucial for Americans mostly because of rules pertaining to exempt and nonexempt workers in the US. You are able to elucidate the overtime regulations and the legal framework. Additionally, you can specify the days when workers receive their pay.

- **Performance management:** This portion trains managers for managerial responsibilities and assists staff members in understanding how their performance will be assessed. You can talk about what you hope managers will do as a team leader and the goals of performance evaluations.

- **Employee development and training:** Here's your opportunity to emphasize a key component of your retention strategy: ensuring that staff members advance both personally and professionally. If there are any, you can discuss budgets for education and training opportunities.

Advantages and Rewards: Has an employee ever said to you something along the lines of, "Wow, I had no idea we had a gym discount"? It's likely that employees frequently don't realize all of the advantages and benefits your business provides. This section aids in maintaining staff awareness of this issue.

Please feel free to add your own special benefits and perks in addition to the following areas found in this benefits and perks template:

- Employee health might include anything from wellness initiatives to gym memberships to private health insurance. Add an explanation of pertinent laws, such as COBRA and FMLA.

- **workers' compensation:** Describe the steps that workers should take in the event that they are hurt at work and the benefits that you will provide. Adjust our template in accordance with local laws that apply.

- **Work from home:** Being able to work from home is becoming more and more of a benefit. Indicate the procedures for employees to request remote work and the guidelines they need abide by (such as at-home cyber security). Include guidelines for employees who work remotely all the time.

- **Employee expenses:** Describe the costs you will pay for and the procedure for filing a claim for reimbursement.

- **Company car:** If you provide employees with company automobiles as a benefit, be careful to let them know what is expected of them when they use them, including what costs (like gas and tolls) you will cover.

- **Parking:** If your workplace provides free parking, teach staff members how to take care of their allotted spot, much like with the company car perk. If there are only a few parking spots available, describe the criteria you will use to distribute them.

- **Equipment provided by the company:** If you provide employees with equipment (such as phones, laptops, etc.), make sure they know how to take care of it. Mention what occurs if the equipment is lost, stolen, or damaged.

Time Off, Vacation, and PTO: Employees will be particularly concerned about this section. They want to know how they can split their time between work and play or after-hours commitments when they join your organization.

Create your own pertinent policies by utilizing this simple-to-edit template that includes the following sections:

- **Hours worked and Paid Time Off (PTO):** Mention the general working hours of your organization and any exclusions. Next, indicate how many paid days off you offer your staff and outline the procedure for submitting a PTO request.

- **Holidays:** Enumerate every holiday that your business observes, and let staff members know how much they will be paid if they must work on these days.

- **Sick leave:** List the benefits that the law requires you to provide to your staff, together with any additional benefits you've chosen to provide. Both the definitions of acute and chronic sickness could be included.

- **Bereavement leave:** Allow employees to take a few days off when a loved one passes away. This is a kind gesture that can build trust between you and your staff.

- **Voting and jury duty:** Explain the laws governing time off for these civic obligations and what paperwork workers may need to bring.

- **Parental leave:** This can refer to legally required maternity and paternity leave as well as company-sponsored leave for staff members who become parents or adopt children. Benefits related to parental allowances, such as a few hours off for attending school meetings, could also be included.

Termination and Resignation of Employees: Employees should understand how their job relationship with your organization will end if things don't work out. particularly in cases where a disciplinary procedure is involved.

This is a template for "leaving the company" that addresses pertinent concerns. This is a summary of the contents:

- **Progressive discipline:** Go over your procedure's steps and the way you anticipate managers handling it.

- **Resignation:** When an employee steps down, they should be aware of the proper resignation procedure and notice time. This is also an excellent time to explicitly forbid forced resignation and discuss other matters such as tuition or relocation reimbursement.

- **Termination:** Describe the relevant legal requirements as well as your internal policy for firing staff members. Talk about the terms of offering severance pay and how you'll make up for any unused sick and vacation time.

- **References:** Include a brief note about providing references to workers who were let go or quit. For instance, you are entitled to decline giving references to an employee who was fired for good reason.

In the end, you might ask staff members to confirm that they have read the handbook and give them advance warning of any upcoming changes.

However, end your employee handbook with a favorable statement. Express your continued happiness that a new hire is joining your team and extend a warm welcome to them. Take inspiration from sample employee handbooks, but remember to write in the voice and style unique to your business.

Creating a Comprehensive Employee Handbook

Eight Essential Elements of a Successful Employee Handbook

1. Be aware of your past: The policies you choose to include in your handbook and the tone it takes will be determined by your company's history, practices, and culture (see below). Additionally, new or updated policies can be required to remain on top of evolving compliance needs. Consider the most important facts to share with staff members, potential areas of miscommunication, and frequently asked questions by staff members.

2. List the necessary policies: While there is no legal requirement for firms to maintain a written employee handbook, there are regulations requiring them to preserve certain policies in writing. For instance, an increasing number of legal jurisdictions mandate that companies uphold written policies regarding workplace safety and health regulations, leave of absence and other time off, harassment, and discrimination. Furthermore, certain information must be included in an employee handbook maintained by a business in accordance with state and municipal legislation. For example, Colorado mandates that companies provide a copy of the Colorado Overtime and Minimum Pay Standards (COMPS) Order (or poster) in their employee handbook. Examine and add to your handbook all the necessary policies that apply to your company.

3. Add any more essential policies: Certain regulations are necessary for communicating crucial information, even in situations when there isn't a formal obligation. Among the instances are:

- A clear at-will clause (with the exception of Montana, where at-will employment is not recognized) at the start of your employee handbook. This is a reminder that, unless there are specific circumstances, you or the employee may end the job relationship at any moment and for any reason.

- Job categories, breaks for meals and rest, payroll and timekeeping, behavior of employees, punctuality, and attendance.

- Leave of absence, nondiscrimination, anti-harassment, and occupational health and safety.

4. Know which policies to stay away from: Knowing which policies to exclude is just as crucial as knowing which ones to include. These include policies that apply universally to criminal convictions, withhold final pay until company property is returned, refuse to pay unpaid overtime or early punch-ins, demand a note from a doctor for each sick day, forbid lawful off-duty behavior, forbid employees from discussing their pay with coworkers, and have English-only or probationary periods.

5. Create draft policies that align with business principles: Many employers have higher expectations than what the law stipulates.

The language employed and the policies chosen can both be seen as reflecting this. For instance, many businesses will define sexual harassment more broadly than what is specified by federal, state, or municipal legislation in order to support the maintenance of a harassment-free workplace.

6. Establish the mood: To help set the tone, employers frequently include a welcome message or section in their handbook. This section of the handbook often offers a synopsis of the company's history, outlines the mission of the organization, highlights its distinctive qualities (such as its work culture and core values), and discusses the significance of the employee handbook.

7. Produce a kind of acknowledgement: It should be mandatory for every worker to sign

and date an admission that they are accountable
for reading, comprehending, and following the
employee handbook. A clause reiterating the
at-will employment relationship should also be
taken into consideration. Describe how the
company reserves the right to amend the
employee handbook at any time and that it is not
a contract for employment. It also explains that
management is still free to interpret policies.

8. Get opinions: After getting input from a
small group of employees on your draft
handbook and acknowledgment form, you
should think about having legal counsel examine
it to make sure it complies with all relevant legal
requirements. While creating your employee
handbook, make preparations for introducing
and distributing it to staff members, teaching
managers on how to interpret and implement the

policies, and updating the handbook whenever company policies or regulations change.

Human Resource Book for Beginners and New
Businesses

CHAPTER 6:

Performance Management

Performance management is a constant discourse that guides people's professional development. It entails setting clear objectives, offering regular feedback, and matching goals to guide staff to success. At its foundation, performance management provides a systematic framework for communication. It establishes goals and expectations, fostering a common understanding of what success looks like. Regular feedback sessions become an essential component, allowing staff to receive assistance, address difficulties, and celebrate accomplishments. Beyond review, performance management is a proactive process that aims to improve. It reveals strengths and opportunities for development, allowing people to improve their talents and make a significant contribution to the team's success. Continuous communication develops a trusting environment, ensuring constructive feedback and individual growth.

In essence, performance management is a dynamic and continuous process that fosters a culture of collaboration and development. It is more than just an assessment tool; it is a way to empower individuals and assist them navigate their professional journeys with clarity and purpose.

Establishing Performance Metrics

As a business owner, you will want to keep an eye on how your company is doing. Keep track of your sales, client satisfaction, and warehouse efficiency. A well-performing firm is one that is profitable. But how do you evaluate performance? So, what are performance metrics? Performance metrics are data used to track business processes. Key metrics used to achieve this include activities, employee behavior, and productivity.Employers then utilize these indicators to evaluate employee performance. This is a reference to a set goal, such as employee productivity or sales targets.

Differentiating Performance Metrics and KPIs?

Performance metrics, or PMs, are measurements of a specific area of an organization. This usually goes against a predetermined goal. This implies you get more data than a key performance indicator (KPI). A KPI will utilize a specific statistic to evaluate performance. For example, a project manager could evaluate the warehousing and shipping department's productivity to a predetermined goal. A key performance indicator (KPI) measures how quickly the warehousing and shipping department can turn an order into a delivery.

Why Monitor Performance Metrics?

Tracking performance metrics is critical since it provides vital information to your company. The data provided by these measures can be used to expand your firm and enhance earnings. They also assist in developing plans for attaining a variety of objectives. This can affect any element of your business. You can plan for enhancements, tweaks, and changes to your company's operations to achieve various objectives.

What Performance Metrics Should I Track?

Businesses employ performance metrics to assess several elements of their operations. This may include sales, project management, personnel productivity, and general corporate procedures.

These measures can be divided into four distinct categories:

- Business Performance
- Sales Performance
- Project management performance
- Employee Performance

Business Performance: Business performance metrics monitor and evaluate how your company performs. This applies to sales, the marketing department, and overall profitability. These measurements assist firms to decide where to make improvements and changes. This is intended to aid improve performance and growth. They will consider factors such as return on investment and profitability of specific aspects. It also focuses on business productivity.

Sales Performance: The sales metrics assess a team's or individual's performance in the sales department. These data can be compared to the target's sales performance, lead generation, and lead retention. It can also analyze critical performance indicators like total revenue and consumer reach. The measures are then compared to the original aims. This allows you, as the business owner, to identify any tendencies of overperformance or underperformance.

Project Management: These metrics are used to monitor and assess the success and profitability of various undertakings. Each stage of the project is tracked and measured against the project's goals. The data gathered from the measurements can be used to plan future initiatives and provide insight into how to make them more efficient.

Employee Performance: The ultimate performance metric is based on employee performance. If your employees fail to meet the criteria set, your business will suffer. However, this is not necessarily due to an individual failing to do their duties correctly. Sometimes they are not given the necessary tools to fulfill their tasks. As a result, these measurements can help you adapt or enhance to assist employees achieve their objectives. You can evaluate an employee's performance based on the quality, quantity, efficiency, and productivity of their job.

Performance metrics are an important tool for any business owner to fine-tune and simplify their operations. To develop an efficient and lucrative firm, everything must run smoothly and at an acceptable level.

Providing Constructive Feedback

Giving someone constructive criticism is similar to giving them a well-made map to help them navigate uncharted territory. It's about pointing people in the direction of a more obvious route for development and progress, not about criticizing them.

First and foremost, specificity is essential: Identify the areas that require acknowledgment or improvement rather than giving general instructions. Particular comments serve as road signs, guiding people toward precisely the areas they should concentrate on.

Time is important: Akin to providing direction at a fork in the road, prompt feedback yields greater results. In order to guarantee that the insights are applicable and pertinent and to support continuous improvement, act quickly to address circumstances.

The important thing is to deliver: Provide feedback in a helpful and encouraging way, much like a kind mentor would. Highlight your positive attributes and present your areas for growth as chances rather than flaws. This strategy makes sure people feel inspired rather than demoralized.

Start a conversation: Establish an open forum for discussion in the same manner that a two-way dialogue promotes understanding. Permit people to contribute their viewpoints and thoughts to create a cooperative environment that promotes development.

Constructive feedback is ultimately a journey toward excellence rather than a critique. It's about giving people the knowledge and skills they need to successfully navigate their professional environment.

Goal Setting for Employees

Employee engagement, motivation, and enthusiasm are essential for starting and running a profitable company. Employees that are satisfied with their work and feel appreciated at work are more productive and drive performance, which in turn benefits the company as a whole. In any industry, managers should place a high premium on fostering employee engagement. Encouraging your employees to define and meet ongoing development goals is one of the simplest and most efficient methods to make them feel motivated and engaged in their work.

However, for employee goal setting to be successful, managers need to do more than merely cross it off their "to-do" list. Let's explore the fundamentals of employee goal-setting and how your company might use this powerful tool.

What is goal setting for employees?

Establishing clear, quantifiable, and role-specific goals for your employees to strive towards during their employment is known as employee goal setting. Employee goals are usually the result of a management and direct report working together. They consider the employee's goals for personal development, the demands of their intended future role, and the availability of resources. The purpose of these work goals is to track employees' performance during the course of their employment with your company, assess their personal growth, and recommend any additional training or upskilling that may be required to meet these objectives. They might be long-term or short-term, and the rewards for finishing them ought to be commensurate with their significance.

The advantages of giving staff goals

There are many advantages to using goal-setting to assist talent development, such as:

- **Enhanced involvement of employees:** Providing your staff with a goal will boost daily workplace engagement, boost motivation, and enhance job performance. By developing their skills, they can attain their objectives.

- **An edge over competitors:** Businesses may gain a competitive edge by investing in employee skill-building, according to 96% of business leaders surveyed by InStride. In the end, skill development and employee objectives that line up with corporate objectives can propel organizational progress.

- Increased retention rates: 94% of departing workers believe they would stay if their employer invested more in employee education. It is evident that including skill development and ongoing education into a goal-setting approach can truly help lower turnover.

Setting goals for employees can be difficult

Although there are many advantages to employee goal planning, there are a few obstacles that may stand in your way. Among the difficulties in establishing goals for employees are:

- unclear goals

- Inconsistency between the company's general strategy and its goals
- unrealistic or unreachable standards
- No way to monitor advancement.

How to set objectives for staff members

Establishing goals for employees is essential for improving individual performance, team cohesion, and eventually business expansion. When setting goals for staff members, keep the following things in mind:

Goals for employees begin at the top: In other words, personal ambitions should coincide with departmental, team, and business goals.

Setting goals is a cooperative process: It is advisable to encourage staff members to participate in creating their own objectives. Team members should be free to contribute to the initiatives they wish to be a part of, but people managers should be available to support and start the process.

Make sure your objectives are quantifiable and reachable: Realistic goals are the only ones that work. Every objective needs to be feasible to accomplish in the allotted time frame.

Put an emphasis on personal development: Creating goals gives staff members a chance to learn more and grow as individuals. Individual career development goals should be brought up during goal-setting discussions.

Forms of frameworks for defining goals for employees

To effectively manage expectations surrounding progress and responsibilities, you may need to, or want to, organize employee goals in a specific way, depending on how your organization handles hierarchy and promotions.

You can use the following kinds of employee goal-setting structures:

Setting OKR Goals: Individuals, groups, or entire organizations use objectives and key results (OKRs) to assign quantifiable goals and set practical tasks. To provide the goal setter(s) with a clear course of action, a goal must include a clearly stated objective and essential results.

The target is a broad aim that establishes particular standards for a particular undertaking. Key results are information or actions taken along the route that show how a group or an individual intends to accomplish the goal.

An illustration of an OKR objective

An example of a personal OKR would be as follows:

- **Goal:** Improve connections with colleagues in various teams.
- **First goal:** Have lunch with a different coworker each week. Second goal: Plan a happy hour.
- **Third key outcome:** Work together across functional lines on a project

MBO Objectives: Management by objectives (MBOs) is a goal-setting technique that uses a rewards-based system to increase engagement and enhance performance for both the organization and its employees. In this model, the manager and direct report collaborate to determine attainable personnel goals that are consistent with the organization's overarching objectives. Reaching these objectives is usually rewarded, either with money or with other kinds of acknowledgment like a promotion or prize. Setting departmental or organizational goals is another usage for MBOs.

SMART Goals Formulation: The acronym SMART refers to precise, measurable, attainable, pertinent, and time-bound. To emphasize the value of assessment in goal-setting, efficacy and feedback (SMARTER) are sometimes added at the end of the acronym. The SMART framework was created to offer precise procedures that would help both individuals and businesses reach their objectives.

Sample of a SMART objective

Let's examine an illustration of a SMART goal:

S — I want to acquire the knowledge and expertise required to advance to the position of HR Director at my business.

M — Before I can become a director, I must finish training courses X, Y, and Z and work as an HR manager.

A — I possess the fundamental knowledge and expertise required, and I have access to ongoing training via my job that will enable me to accomplish this.

R — I am doing well in my current position as an HR specialist, and this career path aligns with both my company's and my own bigger life aspirations.

T — Within the next five years, I hope to finish my master's degree and land the position of HR Manager. I'll be well on my way to becoming HR Director in eight years with this.

Examples of employee goal-setting

Employees can define goals ranging from the highly personal to the organizational using a variety of various "buckets." Employees define role-specific goals based on the positions they now hold or aspire to have within the organization. This kind of objective may focus on productivity, career promotion, or work performance. For instance, a worker in the junior marketing associate position may decide to become a marketing specialist, and to that end, they may devise a plan that includes training, upskilling, and taking on more responsibility. Goals that members of a team or person working together can set for themselves and each other are known as team-specific goals. This makes it easier to plan and assemble your team and makes it obvious what each member's duties and obligations are. For instance, in the next quarter, the marketing team hopes to launch a brand-new social media campaign. In order to make sure that everyone is ready for the launch, the team decides to finish the Instagram marketing short-form certificate.

Employees can create their own personal growth objectives, which don't always have to do with work but can nevertheless boost engagement and job performance. For instance, a worker who wants to spend more time with their family may set a goal to finish work from home by 5:00 p.m. in order to maximize their time there. The requirement for skill improvement runs across all employee goal-setting connected to employment. In order to advance a particular skill set, an employee's goal can call for additional education, training, or even a new degree or certification. Organizations must prioritize skill-building through strategic initiatives that make it possible, such as a workforce education program, in order to assist employees in setting and achieving their goals.

Human Resource Book for Beginners and New
Businesses

CHAPTER 7: Employee Benefits and Engagement

Employee involvement is a word with multiple meanings depending on who you ask. Some may interpret it as passionate employees, while others believe it indicates happy or contented employees. In general, employee engagement refers to people who are dedicated to their jobs as well as their company's aims and ideals. To put it another way, engaged employees show up and participate not only because they are paid to do so, but also because they are emotionally invested.

An organization that promotes and fosters employee involvement will perform better overall. But that's only one motivation to cultivate engaged staff. Here are five other, equally significant reasons why employee involvement is critical.

5 Reasons Why Employee Engagement is Important

1. Engaged staff increase productivity: According to reports, individuals who are committed to their jobs are more productive than those who are not. According to Gallup research, engaged employees are 21% more productive than their disengaged counterparts.

Finding ways to engage your employees, whether through a challenge or additional tasks, means increasing your organization's productivity. In short, it benefits everyone involved.

2. Employee engagement improves consumer satisfaction: People who are enthusiastic about their jobs are frequently the greatest people to interact with your clients. Why? Because that passion is contagious, and your consumers will notice. Quartz claims that the most engaged staff are "more inclined to put in the effort that translates into buzzing productivity levels, a happier sales force, and a more credible product pitch." In other words, engaged staff provide a better client experience. Those who believe in the importance of assisting customers and feel valued by their employer are considerably more likely to provide a positive customer experience and enhance satisfaction.

3. You will keep your finest employees: Employees that are engaged are more committed and invested in their jobs, making them less inclined to quit. Sometimes your finest employees are disengaged and you risk losing them. Keeping people interested is critical to keeping them at your business and producing their best work. If your business is experiencing low retention rates, it's time to investigate why people aren't engaged. Because when the best people in your organization depart, the rest of the team takes note. And you do not want a domino effect.

4. Employee engagement enhances the company culture: People who are enthusiastic about what they do are generally easier to deal with. And not because they are happier or more cheerful. It's because they represent a culture of employee involvement. Ideally, engaged employees live your company's values every day at work and are recognized for it throughout the

160

business. Celebrating your most engaged employees is one step toward fostering an engaging culture.

5. Engagement is an indicator of success: As Ann Latham stated, engagement is a symptom of success. And this does not guarantee commercial success. Rather, engagement is frequently the product of individual or team accomplishment. In other words, engaged employees are motivated not because they are productive or pleasant to work with, but because they believe their work is important. They feel cherished. When their accomplishments are recognized, your employees will believe they have made a significant contribution to the workplace.

Designing Competitive Benefits Packages

In today's competitive business environment, your organization's ability to attract and retain top-tier personnel is vital to its success. A well-designed benefits package is essential in this equation, acting as more than just a recruiting tool. It is an important aspect in creating a culture of employee happiness, engagement, and loyalty. In this expanded essay, we will go deeper into the crucial steps involved in creating a competitive benefits package. We'll look at how this strategic tool may be used to increase your organization's appeal, improve employee well-being, and gain a significant competitive advantage.

1. Understanding Employee Demographics:
The first step in developing a competitive benefits package is to fully understand your employees' demographics. Are they mostly made up of millennials, or do they include the baby boomer generation? What are their lifestyle choices, financial obligations, and professional goals? Answering these questions will assist you in developing a benefits package that is perfectly tailored to the needs and goals of your employees.

For example, younger employees, who are typically saddled with school debt, may benefit greatly from a student loan repayment aid program. Alternatively, more older employees may desire comprehensive health insurance or a strong retirement savings plan. Tailoring your benefits package to address these specific needs increases its appeal and efficacy.

2. The Power of Various Benefits: A really competitive benefits package goes beyond the typical trio of health insurance, vacation days, and retirement savings schemes. Employees in today's workplace expect and value a broader selection of benefits that match their diverse lifestyle and wellness needs. Consider non-traditional benefits such as wellness programs, remote work choices, professional development opportunities, and mental health services. Wellness initiatives have demonstrated efficacy in lowering healthcare expenses, increasing productivity, and improving employee morale. They frequently incorporate workout regimens, nutrition recommendations, stress-management techniques, and regular health checks.

Remote work opportunities are another major lure, allowing people to efficiently combine their professional and home life. Professional development initiatives, such as in-house training, online courses, or tuition reimbursement, can encourage employees to enhance their abilities and advance in their careers.

Recognizing the increase in mental health difficulties, more organizations are providing mental health services. This can include everything from giving access to counseling services to fostering a friendly working culture that values mental health. These programs are not only ethically sound, but they can also considerably boost productivity and employee satisfaction.

3. Keeping up with market trends: Designing a competitive benefits package requires a thorough understanding of market trends. Keeping track of what the top companies in your industry are offering will allow you to benchmark your benefits package and keep it competitive.

However, this does not imply imitating every benefit offered by others. Your company's benefits package should represent its own culture, values, and strategic goals. Use market trends as a guide, not a template, to create a benefits package that is truly unique.

4. Clarity is the Key: Communicate clearly and regularly. A rich benefits package loses its appeal if your employees do not comprehend it. Clear and regular communication about your benefits package is vital. Employees must understand what benefits are available, how they function, and how to take full advantage of them. Communicate your benefits package via a variety of media, including company-wide meetings, thorough benefits guides, FAQ areas on your intranet, regular email updates, and more. Also, consider training your HR team to understand the benefits package. They may then give employees with precise, helpful information, ensuring that the benefits are used effectively and instilling a sense of appreciation and involvement in your team.

5. Regular reviews and revisions: Designing a competitive benefits package is not a one-time activity; it takes ongoing attention and improvement. Market trends vary, employee demands evolve, and business goals change. Regular reviews and adjustments to your benefits package help you to stay current with these developments while keeping your products relevant and successful. Consider holding frequent employee surveys to get input on your benefits package. Their feedback can be quite useful in fine-tuning your products and ensuring they remain appealing and beneficial to your personnel.

6. Leveraging Professional Expertise: Designing a competitive benefits package is a complex process that needs a combination of market research, strategic thinking, and an understanding of human behavior. Engaging expert consulting services can provide your firm with the necessary competitive advantage. Global Healthcare Resources (GHR) offers top-tier wellness consulting services to help firms create competitive benefits packages that correspond with their corporate culture and goals. GHR's experienced consultants provide specific strategies, industry insights, and continuing assistance throughout the implementation process to ensure your benefits package is a viable strategic asset.

GHR's holistic approach to wellness consulting goes beyond simply developing a competitive benefits package. It promotes a culture of employee well-being, increasing productivity and driving corporate success.

Human Resource Book for Beginners and New
Businesses

CHAPTER 8:

Communication and Conflict Resolution

A harmonious workplace is built on effective communication and conflict resolution, which serve as the foundation for collaboration and growth. Consider them as tools in your toolbox for developing good professional relationships. Communication is more than simply words; it is about comprehension, empathy, and clarity. It's like creating a tapestry of connections, with each thread representing a message, concept, or perspective. Clear and open communication creates an environment in which ideas can flow freely, lowering the likelihood of misunderstandings and confrontations.

However, confrontation is unavoidable in every dynamic company. Conflict resolution is not about avoiding problems, but about dealing with them productively. It's similar to being a mediator, finding common ground among opposing viewpoints. Active listening is essential for understanding not only the words stated, but also the emotions and worries that underpin them.

The first step in resolving problems is to acknowledge their presence. It's like casting a light on a dark path; awareness is the first step toward resolution. Creating a comfortable environment for open discourse is critical. This includes encouraging people to voice their opinions and concerns without fear of being judged, so creating a trusting environment.

Human Resource Book for Beginners and New
Businesses

Empathy is what holds conflict resolution together. Understanding other people's viewpoints is similar to walking in their shoes. It promotes a better understanding of other points of view, providing the door for compromise and collaboration. Effective communication and conflict resolution need consistent effort. Regular check-ins, team meetings, and feedback sessions are critical components. It's similar to caring for a garden: constant care results in a healthy and flourishing office environment.

Communication and Conflict Resolution are more than just abilities; they are the foundation of a strong and successful workplace culture. When cultivated and practiced regularly, they create a workplace environment in which employees feel heard, understood, and valued, producing an environment conducive to creativity and achievement.

Open Communication Channels

Open communication channels are essential to a thriving workplace, allowing for a continuous flow of ideas, criticism, and cooperation. Consider them as transparent paths that connect individuals, teams, and leadership, creating an atmosphere in which everyone's voice is heard and respected.

The central theme is transparency: Open communication guarantees that information be openly conveyed, removing hidden barriers. It's like having windows that allow in sunlight, which brightens the team's collective knowledge.

Accessibility is crucial: Just like a well-worn trail is simple to follow, open communication channels should be freely available to all. This accessibility enables people at all levels to share their views, resulting in a varied spectrum of perspectives.

Feedback is an essential component: It is not enough to simply transmit messages; it is also necessary to receive and act on them. Consider it a two-way street, with constructive criticism and positive reinforcement paving the path for ongoing improvement.

Regular check-ins function as checkpoints along this communication highway: These encounters, whether in team meetings or one-on-one sessions, function as road signs, providing direction and ensuring that everyone is on the same page.

Empathy is the link that binds people: Open communication channels enable people to comprehend and appreciate different points of view. It is about recognizing that each voice is unique and adds to the colorful tapestry of the workplace.

Creating open communication channels necessitates dedication: It's a continuous process, similar to caring for a garden that needs frequent attention. Regular updates, transparent policies, and a culture that promotes open dialogue all contribute to the success of these channels.

Open communication channels are the lifeblood of a thriving workplace, encouraging the interchange of ideas and fostering a feeling of community. When developed, they allow individuals to express themselves, share their knowledge, and contribute to the team's overall success.

Maintaining a Positive Work Environment

Maintaining a positive work atmosphere is critical to increasing productivity and employee well-being. It demands creating an open communication culture in which team members feel heard and valued. Clear expectations lay a firm foundation for avoiding uncertainty and promoting a feeling of direction.

- Recognition is essential for inspiring people. Regular recognition of their work promotes a positive attitude and dedication to excellence. Flexible work arrangements meet a wide range of needs, making the workplace more adaptive and robust.

- Collaboration is essential to unleashing creativity. Encouraging teamwork and cross-functional relationships facilitates the interchange of ideas, resulting in innovative solutions. Maintaining a balance between work and personal life is critical for general health and avoiding burnout.

Maintaining a positive work environment requires effective communication, clear expectations, recognition, flexibility, and teamwork. When these factors are highlighted, the workplace becomes a place where people may thrive, which contributes to a positive and successful culture.

Human Resource Book for Beginners and New Businesses

CHAPTER 9: Continuous Learning and Development

Continuous learning and development are like the chapters of a fascinating book that shape your personal and professional life. It is not a static condition, but rather a continual process of discovery and progress, with each experience and skill obtained adding to your ongoing story.

- Being curious and open-minded is at the heart of lifelong learning. It is about approaching challenges with the mindset of an adventurer, eager to uncover new ideas and broaden your horizons. Just as a visitor explores uncharted territory, you welcome opportunities to expand your knowledge and expertise.

- Professional development is like creating a masterpiece. It entails deliberately honing your skills, devoting time to improving your abilities, and remaining responsive to the demands of your changing field. This devotion guarantees that you not only keep up with the present, but also remain ahead of the curve by anticipating and reacting to future issues.

- Adaptability is a natural outcome of this journey. In a world that is continuously changing, the capacity to pivot and welcome new methods is critical. It's like having an adaptable toolkit that allows you to negotiate uncertainty, take opportunities, and thrive in a changing environment.

- In this mission, technology will be your ally. Using online classes and interactive platforms is like having a library of information at your fingertips. The digital landscape enables rapid access to a plethora of information, facilitating your ongoing learning journey.

- Collaboration is an essential component of this journey. Engaging with peers, mentors, and industry networks is similar to embarking on a group excursion. Shared experiences and insights not only help you learn, but they also generate a sense of community and support.

Ongoing learning and development are the narrative threads that connect your tale of growth. Embracing this approach guarantees that you not only negotiate the twists and turns of your trip, but also contribute to the bigger picture, leaving an unforgettable stamp on your personal and professional environment.

Importance of Continuous Learning

Continuous learning is like having an endless source of inspiration and growth in your life. It's more than just learning new skills; it's a mindset that pulls you forward, keeping you current, engaged, and fulfilled in your personal and professional endeavors.

- At its essence, continuous learning is about maintaining curiosity. It is a commitment to asking questions, seeking answers, and enjoying the thrill of discovery. It's like beginning on an endless adventure of exploration, enriching your perspective and keeping your mind flexible and open to new ideas.

- Continuous learning is extremely important in the professional world. The world is changing at an unprecedented rate, and staying current takes more than a static set of abilities. It's about being ahead of the curve, embracing new technologies, and being open to novel ways.

- Continuous learning is an investment in oneself. It acknowledges that your potential for advancement and impact is infinite. Actively searching out opportunities to learn, whether through formal education, on-the-job experiences, or self-directed exploration, prepares you to negotiate the intricacies of an ever-changing environment.

Furthermore, continuous learning provides a sense of empowerment. It allows you to direct your own development and career path. Instead of being a passive bystander, you take an active role in crafting your destiny, prepared to seize opportunities and conquer obstacles. Continuous learning is more than a habit; it's a lifestyle. It ensures that you are not just surviving, but thriving, always increasing your capabilities and making important contributions to the world around you. It represents a dedication to lifelong learning and an understanding that the journey of learning is just as important as the result.

Implementing Ongoing Training Initiatives

An employee training implementation plan is an essential component of any successful firm, especially during the onboarding of new employees. If suitable training is not provided, the efforts may be wasted. In contrast, effective training initiatives can set employees on the path to success.

Employers can make a number of blunders when planning staff training initiatives, such as adopting obsolete and boring training methods.

When training is not properly designed, it frequently fails to meet the expectations of participants and organizational objectives.

An employee training implementation plan is an essential component of any successful firm, especially during the onboarding of new employees. If suitable training is not provided, the efforts may be wasted. In contrast, effective training initiatives can set employees on the path to success.

In today's remote working world, it is critical to have continual training that may be offered online. The staff training initiative program should be developed using a step-by-step, systematic approach.

Here are seven approaches to implement successful employee training initiatives:

Establish goals that are linked with employee needs and company requirements: Training is crucial not only for your workforce, but also for the growth of your organization. Your company's efficiency increases as your staff become more dedicated, engaged, and skilled. Having outstanding subscription services, heaps of books, and free courses is pointless if your business objectives do not line with employee and corporate needs.

When establishing staff training programs with the company's aim and vision in mind, you will be able to:

- Provide a strategic method for investing in your training activities.

- Get a clear picture of what you can achieve after investing in training programs.
- Provide relevant training opportunities for your personnel. This improves their job performance.

Bring employees on board and solicit recommendations: You must give your staff an environment in which their opinions are heard. Listen to your employees' ideas and disagreements to build a strong corporate culture. According to research, 65% of employees do not engage because they believe they cannot ask their boss any questions. Also, 75% of employees want to stay with a company that understands and addresses their problems.

All of your employees require balanced and regular feedback, particularly when conducting training projects. Feedback is required so that your employees may match their performance with the organizational culture. You should discuss areas for improvement and applaud behavior that aligns with your company's ideals. Effective training and development techniques require a systematic approach to curriculum creation. It should be designed so that it motivates people to collaborate toward a common goal.

Furthermore, it should detail the actions required to increase employee engagement levels at each training step. Aim to foster a learning culture that prioritizes self-development and team improvement. Create a program that addresses the needs of all employees. When it comes to training and development, similarly, understand cultural differences and develop a common language.

Ensure employee training aligns with consumer needs: Whether they be external or internal clients, employee training activities should ultimately result in customer satisfaction. Positive customer experiences improve customer retention and expand the customer base. Therefore, avoid focusing solely on work procedures and processes. Work on teaching staff so that they comprehend your products and services. Make them feel confident that they can learn to communicate with customers in an efficient and comfortable manner.

Break down your staff training plan into smaller, more manageable aims: This helps you determine whether you are achieving the intended results at each step of the program. It also aids in identifying flaws and opportunities for improvement in your training implementation strategy.

Some of the key classic aspects that distinguish training strategy include:

- A clear declaration of objectives and proposed deliverables.
- Detailed investigation of training benefits to evaluate ROI.
- Designing surveys to gather feedback from learners
- Creating a realistic training budget that includes all necessary expenses
- Set a timeframe for each section of employee training. Before beginning the

training, determine how much time is required to finish each program segment.

Your training material and style of delivery also influence how much time you need to complete the program. Remember to make training methods interesting and engaging, and set a reasonable deadline for completion. With a suitable schedule, your employees can plan for attending training. When each training goal is completed within a specific time limit, employee motivation increases and results improve.

Hire expert instructors for training: On-the-job training typically produces outstanding outcomes when properly equipped and delivered by skilled teachers. However, it is critical not to overwhelm your employees with information on the first day. However, provide just-in-time training when they are ready to apply the material.

Implement standardized training methods: Employees generally find training useless or uninteresting. Even if they attend the training session, they lose interest. The fundamental cause for such unsuccessful training approaches is a failure to meet the learner's needs.

This emphasizes the need of designing training approaches that provide knowledge in the most effective style for learners. Some of the standard training methods are:

- E-Learning
- Instructor-led training
- Training involves hands-on activities and lectures.

- Coaching or Mentoring
- Engage in role-playing and group discussions.
- Studying real-life scenarios and case studies.

You can select one or more training techniques based on the employees' learning requirements and training objectives.

Increase Training Flexibility: Your organization may have employees ranging from mid-20s to late 30s, with diverse interests. Some employees may prefer mobile training sessions, whereas others prefer a classroom setting. To ensure that every team member is satisfied, it is critical to incorporate various learning styles into your training activities.

According to McKinley's research, 55% of employees prefer a flexible working environment as part of their package. Using standard training tools can be challenging for training both new and existing staff, especially in a rapidly changing company environment. The next stage is to select training tools that make training information easily accessible to learners. Choosing innovative tools is a financial decision, since your organization must invest wisely in its training resources. This manner, you may keep training costs under control.

Human Resource Book for Beginners and New
Businesses

CONCLUSION

In conclusion, this book has been a dynamic investigation of numerous human resource subjects, ranging from recruitment strategies to dispute resolution procedures. It reflects the varied range of obstacles and opportunities that individuals, particularly beginners and those starting new businesses, may face in the field of human resources.

Throughout the book, the emphasis has been on clarity and simplicity, with the goal of providing practical insights and human-centered approaches. We've covered the nuances of continual learning, the value of happy work environments, and the fundamental ideas required for effective HR management.

As the book finishes, it represents a snapshot of shared learning and direction. Whether delving into the complexities of HR basics, discussing recruitment nuances, or investigating the mechanics of dispute resolution, the goal has been to provide simple and human-friendly insights.

Communication, as in HR practices, has been a key element in creating understanding and answering questions. The journey through this book exemplifies the notion of continual learning, adapting to your needs while delivering practical insights to help you understand HR subjects. Remember that the human element is at the heart of HR, and this book has attempted to bring that perspective to life. Whether you're new to the field or navigating the complexities of human resources in a new company venture, the ideas offered here are intended to be a useful companion on your journey.

Promoting continuous learning in HR for new firms is like planting the seeds for future growth. It entails building an environment in which HR professionals remain interested and learning-oriented throughout their careers. To begin with, encouraging curiosity is crucial. HR professionals, like explorers on their quest for discovery, should be keen to learn about emerging trends and practices. Consider creating an easily accessible repository for learning materials. Making these resources available, whether through online courses or articles, allows HR professionals to stay up to date and improve their abilities.

Supporting personalized development plans is similar to giving individuals their own developmental path. It helps them determine the talents they wish to learn and ensures that they are in line with the company's requirements. Encouraging learning from multiple sources is analogous to examining different regions of a garden for new viewpoints. HR workers might benefit from cross-functional training to expand their skill set. Recognizing successes is similar to appreciating blooming flowers. Celebrating achievements like certificates or great performance encourages HR professionals to continue their learning path.

Creating a learning community where information can be shared is similar to having a group of buddies at work who encourage one another and study together. Leadership is essential, just as a seasoned gardener is responsible for his or her garden. Leaders in the HR team should demonstrate a commitment to learning by inspiring others and emphasizing the importance of continuous learning for everybody.

Human Resource Book for Beginners and New
Businesses

REVIEW PAGE

Dear Reader,

I hope everything is good with you. I'm writing to respectfully ask that you evaluate Human Resource Books for Beginners and New Businesses.

We value your comments much and will use it to keep improving and provide the best. We will be able to better understand what is functioning well and pinpoint areas where we can improve the overall experience with the aid of your opinions and views.

We sincerely value your time and participation, whether it is in the form of compliments or recommendations for development. Your frank assessment will help us improve greatly.

We appreciate your continued support and your status as an important part of our community. We anticipate speaking with you.

Warm regards,

Francis A. Wiles

Human Resource Book for Beginners and New
Businesses